Welcome to the fun of drinking and color

In this book you will find 20 Gin co

Cocktails that will provide you with some interesting taste sensations.

For each cocktail there are 2 coloring sheets.

Remove the one without a name to color in with your friends as you try that cocktail. Get them to guess the name of the cocktail based on the background - You might even make up better names.

I hope this book brings you a good evening, filled with laughter and you impress your guests with your cocktail making skills.

Cocktail Menu

1   Bee's Knees
2   Gin Basil Smash
3   Clover Club
4   Millionaires Martini
5   French 75
6   London Calling
7   Bramble
8   The Last Word
9   Martinez
10   Aviation
11   Satan's Whiskers
12   Angels' Advocate
13   Cosmonaut
14   Cowboy Hoof Martini
15   The Money Penny
16   Banana Calling
17   Breakfast Martini
18   Glass & Bottle
19   Fruit Cup
20   Angel Face

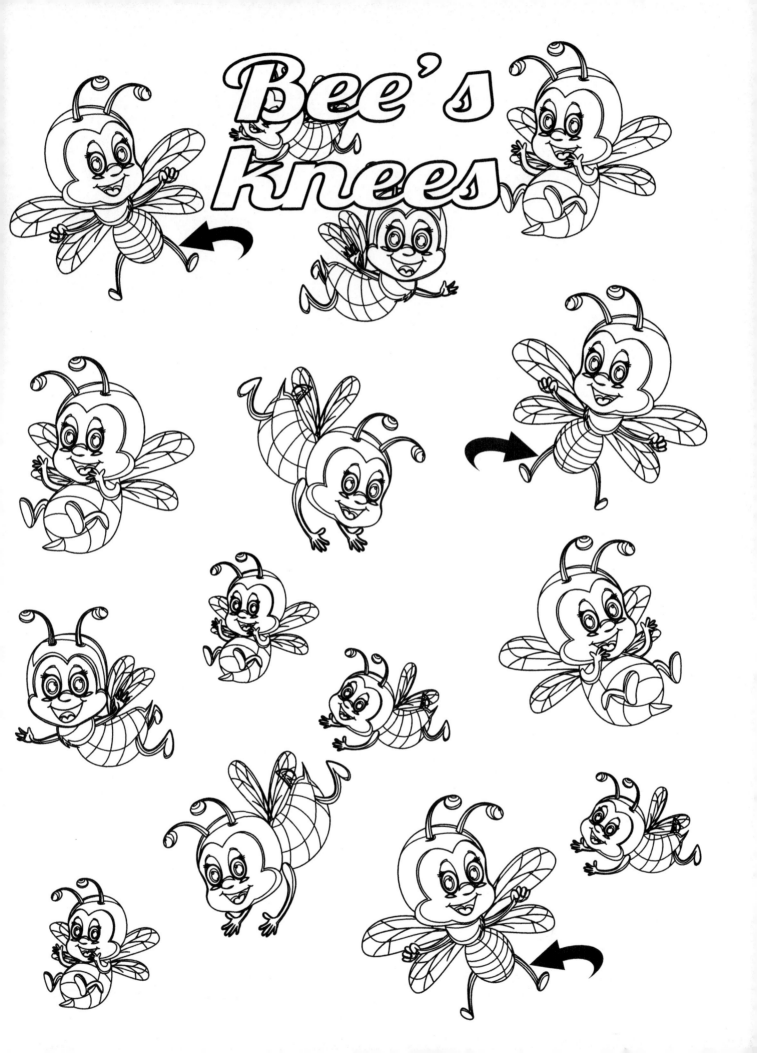

Ingredients

50ml Gin

2 teaspoons Honey

20ml Lemon juice

20ml Orange juice

Garnish - an orange twist

Mixing

Combine gin & honey in a cocktail shaker & stir well to dissolve the honey.

Add the citrus juices & fill the shaker with ice.

Shake well.

Double strain into a chilled glass.

Ingredients

50ml Gin
15ml Lemon juice
10ml Sugar syrup
6 - 12 Basil leaves
Garnish - basil leaves

Mixing

Muddle basil leaves in a cocktail shaker.

Add ice & other ingredients.

Shake well.

Double strain into an ice filled glass.

Ingredients

50ml Gin

10ml Lemon juice

5ml Grenadine or raspberry syrup

10ml Sweet vermouth

Handful of fresh raspberries

1 egg white

Garnish with a raspberry

Mixing

Dry shake all the ingredients until the egg has emulsified and the berries have been pulverised.

Add half a cup of ice.

Shake again until cold.

Fine strain into a chilled coupe glass.

Ingredients

40ml Gin

40ml Dry vermouth

Champagne

Mixing

Combine the gin & vermouth in an ice filled mixing glass.

Stir until properly chilled.

Strain into a chilled coupe glass

&

Top with champagne.

Ingredients

35ml Gin
20ml Lemon juice
10ml Sugar syrup
Champagne
Garnish - strip of lemon zest

Mixing

Combine the gin, lemon juice & sugar syrup in an ice filled cocktail shaker.

Shake well.

Strain into a champagne flute.
Top with chilled champagne.

Ingredients

45ml Gin
15ml Fino sherry
10ml Lemon juice
7.5ml Sugar syrup
2 dashes orange biters
Garnish - grapefruit zest twist

Mixing

Shake all the ingredients with ice.
Fine strain into a chilled glass.

Ingredients

50ml Gin

10ml Sugar syrup

20ml Lemon Juice

20ml Sloe gin or Crème de mure

Garnish - blackberry & fresh lemon slice

Mixing

Put the 1st 3 ingredients in a glass with ice & stir.

Top with crushed ice.

Drizzle over either the sloe gin or crème de mure for the float.

The Last Word

Ingredients

30ml Gin
25ml Chartreuse
20ml Luxardo Maraschino liqueur
20ml Fresh lime juice
Garnish - a cherry

Mixing

Shake all the ingredients with ice.
Strain into a chilled coupe glass.

Martinez

Ingredients

60ml Gin
25ml Sweet Vermouth
25ml Dry Vermouth
1 dash Angostura bitters
2 dashes Maraschino liqueur
Garnish - lemon or orange twist

Mixing

Stir all the ingredients with ice.
Strain into a chilled glass.

Ingredients

52.5ml Gin

15ml Luxardo Maraschino liqueur

7.5ml Crème de Violette liqueur

15ml Lemon juice

Mixing

Shake all the ingredients with ice.

Fine strain into a chilled glass

Ingredients

20ml Gin
20ml Martini extra dry vermouth
20ml Martini rosso sweet vermouth
10ml Grand Marnier liqueur
20ml Orange juice
1 dash orange bitters
Garnish - orange zest twist

Mixing

Shake all the ingredients with ice.
Fine strain into a chilled glass.

Ingredients

45ml Gin
5ml Advocaat liqueur
15ml Monin Vanilla syrup
20ml Lemon juice
1 dash Bob's cardamon bitters
Garnish - orange zest twist

Mixing

Shake all the ingredients with ice.
Fine strain into a chilled glass

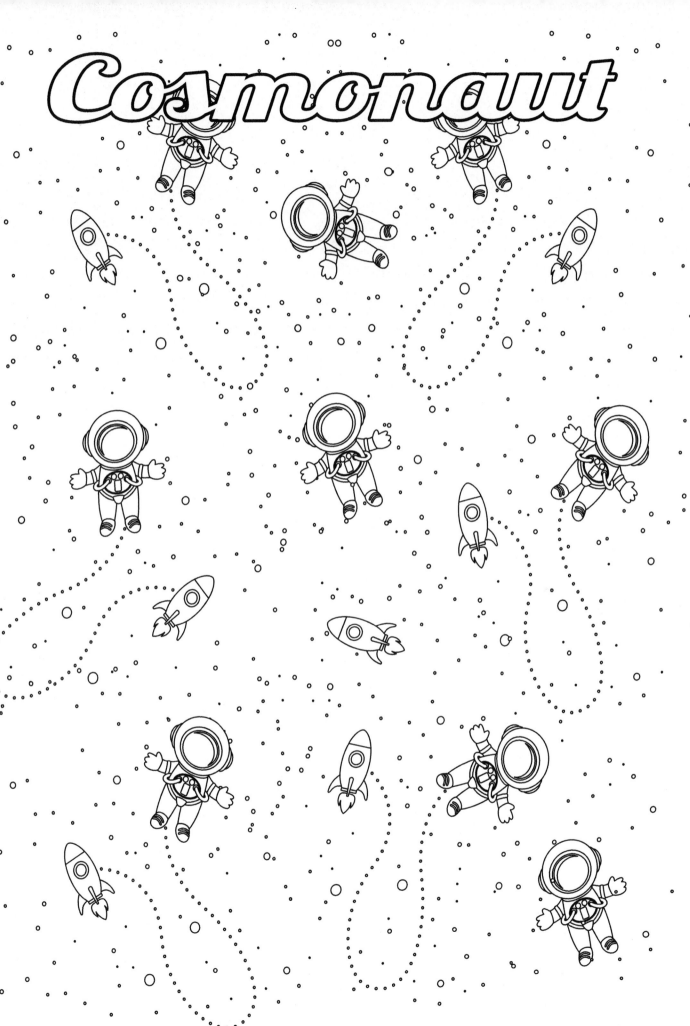

Ingredients

60ml Gin

22.5ml Lemon juice

3 teaspoons raspberry jam

Garnish - fresh raspberry

Mixing

Stir all the ingredients together in the base of a shaker to dissolve the jam.

Shake with ice.

Fine strain into a chilled glass.

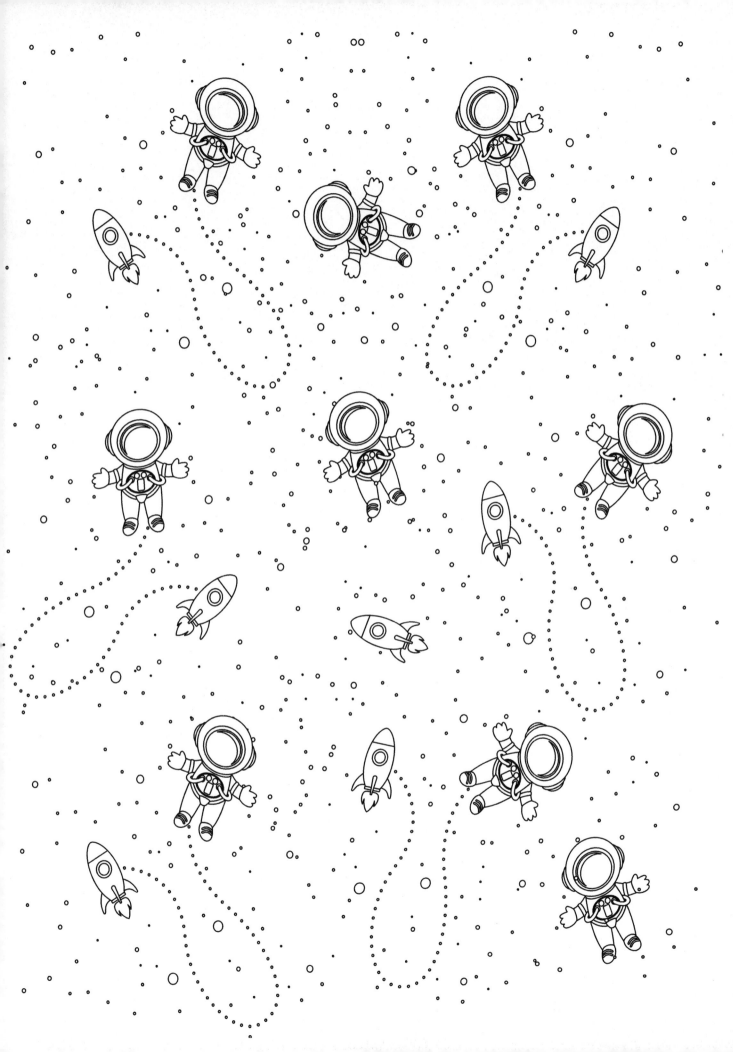

Ingredients

5 fresh mint leaves

75ml Gin

5ml Sugar syrup

2 dashes Orange bitters(optional)

Garnish - orange zest twist

Mixing

Shake all the ingredients, including the mint leaves, with ice.

Fine strain into a chilled glass

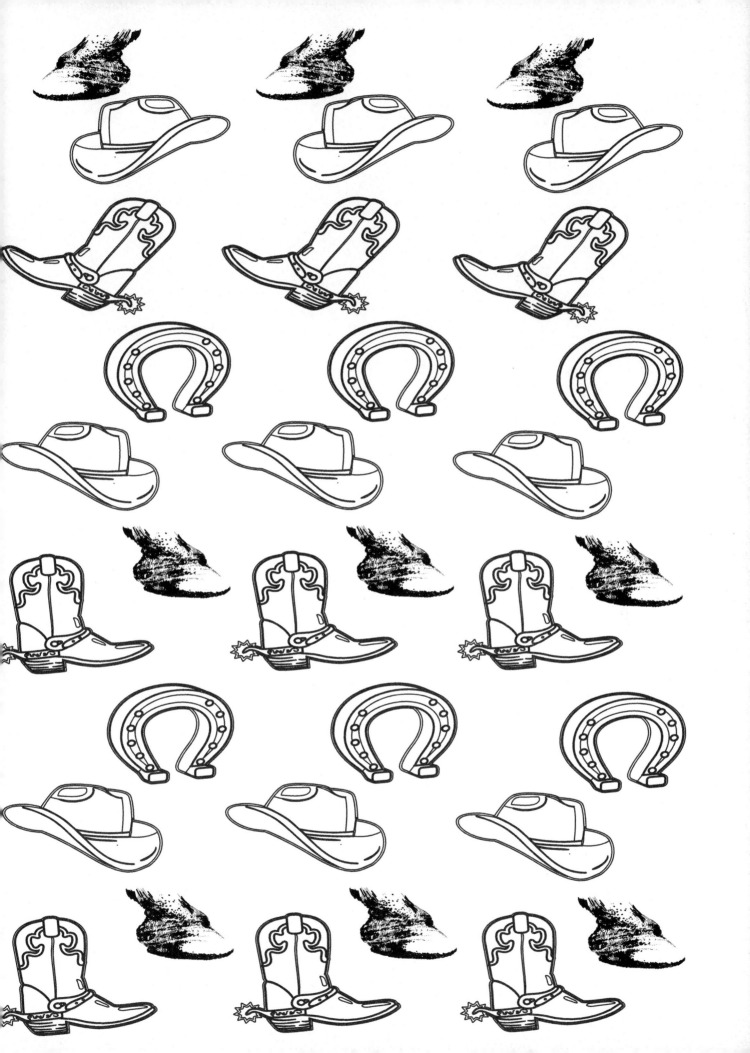

Ingredients

60ml Gin

22.5ml Pink grapefruit juice

15ml Martini extra dry vermouth

7.5ml Sugar syrup

1 dash Bob's grapefruit bitters.

Garnish - grapefruit zest twist

Mixing

Shake all the ingredients with ice.

Fine strain into a chilled glass.

Ingredients

50ml Gin

12.5ml Gifford Banane du Bresil

10ml Fino Sherry

25ml Lemon juice

10ml Sugar syrup

Mixing

Shake all the ingredients with ice.

Fine strain into a chilled glass.

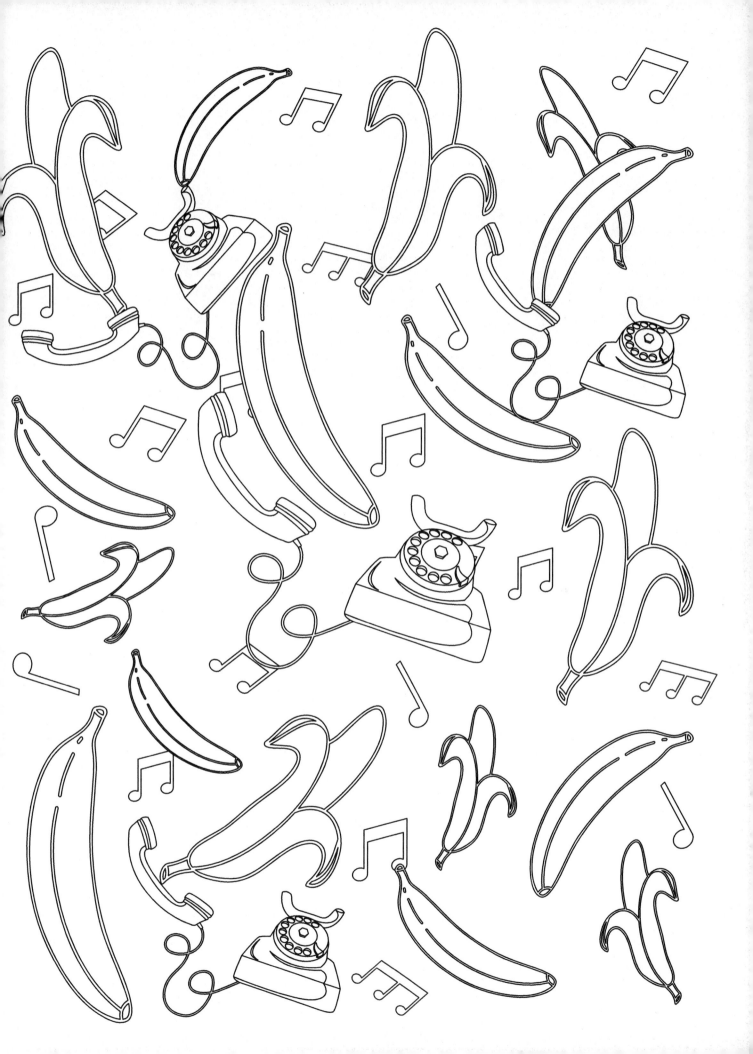

Ingredients

1 spoon orange marmalade

50ml Gin

15ml Triple Sec (40%)

15ml Lemon juice

Garnish - orange zest twist & a mini slice of toast

Mixing

Stir the marmalade with the gin in the base of a shaker until it dissolves.

Add the other ingredients.

Shake with ice.

Fine strain into a chilled glass.

Ingredients

30ml Gin

15ml Suze Gentian liqueur

22.5ml Americano Bianco

5ml Sugar syrup

22.5ml Lemon Juice

1 pinch of salt.

Garnish - salted cucumber wheel

Mixing

Shake all the ingredients with ice.

Strain into a chilled glass

Fruit Cup

Ingredients

25ml Gin

25ml Orange Curacao liqueur

25ml Martini rosso sweet vermouth

2 dashes Angostura bitters

50ml Ginger ale

50ml Cola

Garnish - lemon, orange & strawberry slices, mint sprig & borage in drink.

Mixing

Pour all the ingredients into a glass.

Half fill the glass with ice.

Add a citrus slice & a couple of mint leaves.

Fill the glass to the top with ice.

Ingredients

30ml Gin
30ml Calvados
30ml Apricot brandy
10ml Chilled water

Garnish - orange zest or apple wedge
on rim

Mixing

Stir all the ingredients with ice.
Fine strain into a chilled glass.

Printed in Great Britain
by Amazon